I'm A Sunshine Guy
The Life Story of Edmond R. Gaines

EDMOND R. GAINES
and
SUMMER GAASEDELEN

Cover photo: Edmond R. Gaines with friend Tom Gilsenan, executive director of Uptown Bill's Extend the Dream Foundation at Uptown Bill's Coffeeshop. Ed selected this photo for the cover of his life story because he loves to spend time at Uptown Bill's surrounded by friends. Photo credit: Maria Ortega Kummer.

ISBN-10: 1724667351
ISBN-13: 978-1724667359

*To my dad and mom, who gave me the tools
to become independent.* —E.R.G.

CONTENTS

ACKNOWLEDGMENTS

Thank you to Ed and Barbara for the many hours
they spent telling me Ed's story, going through photographs,
and making sure that this book provides a good and accurate
representation of Ed's life. –S.G.

1

I emailed Ed to tell him how sorry I was for forgetting to come and make dinner for him. He responded, "It's okay. I had Pop-Tarts for dinner! HAHAHA!"

I met Ed while I was working as a caretaker for people with disabilities in Iowa City. He has cerebral palsy, a lifelong physical disability. He also has a severe hearing impairment. I helped him with his household chores, health, and hygiene. He was 64 at the time. He wore a Hawkeye sweatshirt and cap. His beard was long. He almost always had Mountain Dew in hand.

Until Hostess announced that it would be shutting down all of its factories at the end of 2012, Ed would routinely request bologna and American cheese on Wonder Bread for lunch. If I bought enriched Wonder Bread, Ed could taste it and would remind me to get original next time. He kept model cars and loved Andy Griffith. He was a child of the 1950s.

The day he asked me to write his life story, our routine tasks were moving slower than usual. I remember being surprised that Ed asked me to write his story, because he had already written it in a piece titled "The Physical Pest: The True Story of a Man with Cerebral Palsy," along with several poems. I agreed, as long as I could include excerpts of his writing.

Sixty-Four
By Edmond R. Gaines
Written for the occasion of his 64th birthday

What is sixty-four?
Is it your birthday?
OH! I get it!
It is a chessboard
That has 64 squares!

There are sixteen soldiers
Eight men each support
Their seven strong lords
And a powerful queen

Their lords are
two elevated Rooks,
two crooked Knights,
two uglihead Bishops
And, of course, a shy King

What is their goal?
Their goal is,
Their secret strategies,
On the sixty-four squares,
Of big green and white chessboard,
One person shouts!
"Checkmate, baby!!!"

Chess is Ed's lifelong passion. He is a certified life member of the U.S. Chess Federation, whose mission is "to empower people through chess one move at a time." For Ed chess is about enriching life and community. He's also a tough competitor.

Ed won the reserve division of the U.S. Chess Federation tournament in Iowa City in 1992. He has also competed at the national level in Chicago and Las Vegas.

While serving as a board member at The Iowa State Chess Association Corporation, Ed helped to organize chess events and connected with other Iowa chess enthusiasts. Ed was a vital member of the University of Iowa club before the Iowa Flood of 2008, which affected most of the rivers in eastern Iowa. The flood caused such damage to the university club's facilities that the club closed.

"I am very patient," Ed says. Patience, he tells me, is the secret to his success in chess and to his contagious happiness.

Ed continues to engage in game strategy through online chess and Words with Friends. He also continues to challenge friends and acquaintances to rounds of chess.

Ed learned chess at the University of Iowa Hospital School for Handicapped Children in Iowa City. Though his records from the hospital school indicate that he wasn't always so patient. Or as Ed puts it, "I was a troublemaker."

At the hospital school Ed wore 1.25 lb. shoe weights, 2.5 lb. arm weights, and hearing aids. The arm weights were to train him to keep his arms down. Without the weights, his arms would stay close to his chest or flail during the convulsions caused by cerebral palsy. The shoe weights helped him to maintain balance as he was learning to walk. The phrase "Eddie continues to reject his appliances," occurs regularly throughout the hospital school medical notes.

Ed's classroom at the University of Iowa Hospital School. Ed can be seen at the far left of the photograph. Gaines family photo collection.

Ed started school in 1954 when he was 5 years old. When he arrived, his only form of locomotion was rolling across the floor. The hardest part of being at school was being far away from his family. The hospital school was in Iowa City, but Ed's family lived 79 miles away in Burlington, Iowa.

Throughout his nine years at the hospital school, Ed's mother, Lillian Alvara Gaines, found flexible jobs including one as an office worker in an advertising firm. Her job allowed her the time she needed to drive to Iowa City and bring Ed home for the weekend every six weeks. Having Ed far away was difficult on the family, but in the 1950s, resources for children with cerebral palsy were few and hard to find.

Finding the hospital school was a major breakthrough for the Gaines family. Ed's parents had sought help to provide for Ed's needs from the very beginning, but did not find any resources in Quincy, Illinois, where Ed was born in 1948. Ed's father, Richard Floyd Gaines, and Lillian took Ed to a brain and spine specialist in Quincy. They were told to "take him home and let him go." In other words, the doctors did not see any hope of Ed learning to walk or talk. Nonetheless, Ed's parents continued to hold on to hope and consult with doctors. Among the Gaines' family collection of newspaper articles written about Ed's life, Richard is quoted as saying, "I would have consulted a witch doctor if I thought it would do any good."[i]

Dr. Robert Bruner of Kansas City and his staff were the first specialists who offered the Gaines family help. Ed was 4 years old at the time and the family had already moved to Burlington, Iowa, for Richard's work. Rather than treating Ed's case as hopeless, Dr. Bruner's team gave the family suggestions that would help Ed learn to walk and talk at his own pace. To start, a nurse noticed that Ed did not move his tongue from corner to corner, so she put peanut butter in the corner of his mouth to help improve his tongue movements. Most importantly, it was Dr. Bruner who recommended the hospital school in Iowa City.

Once the Gaines family found the specialized care they needed, Ed began on the path to independence.

Ed describes his first days at the hospital school in "The Physical Pest":

> They tried to stand me up but I fell down suddenly. The physical therapist worked with me on standing up. At first for five seconds a couple days, then fifteen seconds, and then thirty seconds. After a while I began to walk. The speech therapists also worked with me when I was about six years old. It took a long time for me to talk

4

because of my hearing and speech impediments. Reading people's lips took me even longer. Walking and talking were the first main things to do before I started to do anything else.

Ed's family maintained a positive relationship with the school. Hospital notes describe his parents as "Interested. Intelligent. Realistic."

The hospital school taught Ed to be independent 5-seconds at a time. Physical therapists would help Ed into a standing position and encourage him to remain standing for just 5 seconds. When he accomplished it, the 5 became 15 seconds until Ed could stand alone. He eventually learned how to walk and speak at the hospital school.

By the time he graduated from the hospital school, he had also learned to express what he could and couldn't do. Ed gives the example, "I can't hear, but I can read lips." Recognizing and expressing this distinction was vital to Ed's communication with others who would look away or avoid eye contact while speaking.

Learning independence continued at home. In a newspaper article Lillian was quoted as saying, "We worked faithfully with the hospital school. When they told us to let him tie his shoes, we did, even if it took an hour. The same was true with buttoning his shirt."[ii]

The University of Iowa Hospital School for Handicapped Children opened October 13, 1948. The school was the first initiative in Iowa for severely handicapped children. It was designed for children who were physically handicapped and denied access to public schools, but who had "normal intelligence." The funding for the hospital school was given in response to efforts from the parents of handicapped children appealing to the state government.[iii]

In the beginning, the hospital school had a small amount of funding and was housed in the basement of a university hall. By 1954 the program grew into a new facility that could accommodate 60 students with an industrial arts shop, gymnasium, cafeteria, playground, and wading pool.

That facility now houses the Center for Disabilities, where Ed goes for wheelchair evaluation. Former resident rooms are now offices and labs, and the former sunroom that once had a grand piano, fireplace, and couches for families to visit residents is now a center for sleep study.

During Ed's time at the hospital school, he received special education, physical education, and education in communication skills, industrial arts, homemaking, and music. The students also received healthcare from physical therapists, nurses, and professionals from a variety of specialized fields.

While the children learned life skills, researchers observed their movements using motion picture x-rays, seeking information that could be generalized to all children with physical disabilities. Ed's hospital notes indicate that his speech patterns were evaluated:

> Motion picture x-rays were made of Ed's palate and tongue movements during connected speech. Gross inspection of the film indicated that he was obtaining closure of the velo-pharyngeal port. Whether or not the closure was timed appropriately for speech has not yet been determined. The film also indicated that he was humping the back of the tongue so as to contact the soft palate.

Doctors determined that Ed required a pharyngeal flap procedure to correct his airflow during speech. Throughout his time at the hospital school, he received four half-hour sessions of individual speech therapy weekly. In these sessions, Ed worked on pronunciation and increasing his vocabulary.

After a few years at the hospital school, Ed's parents wanted him to attend the public school in Burlington. His hospital notes document their hopes (and a glimpse at his relationship with his sisters):

> We discussed public school possibilities for Ed. Parents are hopeful he may attend public school next fall. The school Ed would attend is one block from their home. He would have many steps to manage (about a dozen to go up when entering, two flights to manage to get to the toilets in the basement.) Mother will check to determine if there are possibly toilet facilities on 1st floor for the K group of children. She also will attempt to discover what speech help might be present in the local system. Linda is presently in Gr VI and will be leaving this school in June. Barbara is in Gr IV now and Ed's possible placement should take this into consideration. She has been the most overprotective member of the family in her "mothering" of Ed.

Lillian's and Richard's hopes to have Ed attend the local school were not fulfilled, as the public school in Burlington would not accept a child with disabilities. Iowa public schools were not required to accept children with disabilities until the Federal Rehabilitation Act of 1973 came into effect.

Ed stayed at the hospital school for nine years. Ed's teachers and nurses knew him well, and some worked with him for his entire time at the hospital school. In a note to the faculty, Ed's speech coach encouraged his teachers not to allow that familiarity to get in the way of his speech education:

> Do not respond to Ed's poor speech attempts. If he feels he can continue to obtain the attention of people with poor speech, he will have no real desire for speaking better.

While his hospital notes suggest that speaking clearly was one of his biggest struggles, Ed's mathematics teacher said, "Eddie is very accurate in arithmetic and shows particular pride and interest in this area."

By the end of his time at the hospital school, Ed had gained enough physical control to do well in industrial arts, where he successfully maneuvered power machinery:

> At the present, Ed is finishing up a wooden tie holder. He used the power machinery to aid in construction. He did an excellent job on the jig-saw and therefore it didn't take him long to complete the project.

The highlight of Ed's years at the hospital school was the school's 1960 production of "The Mikado," a comic opera with music by Arthur Sullivan and libretto by W. S. Gilbert. Ed played a guard and the production was televised.

When Ed was 14 years old, he left the hospital school. He says, "After nine years in this wonderful school, I went into the reality for the first time. I went to junior high school." His sister, Barbara, says it was because he had learned everything they could teach him there. Ed says people left the hospital school around 13 because that's when they started smoking. He adds "I only had one puff of a cigarette."

Following several legislative acts in the 1970s, including "The Education For All Handicapped Children Act" in 1975, which stated that all children had a right to receive education in their home communities, the hospital school slowly converted from a boarding school to a resource center for outclinic and outreach services for community programs.

Ed started at James Madison Junior High school in 1963 in Burlington after his mother lobbied the principal. Though Ed was able to continue his education there, he says "the people were afraid of me because of my disability, and I didn't know why." Neither the other students nor the teachers were used to being around people with disabilities. Ed was also older than his peers, since he did not enroll in junior high until he was 14 years old.

Even with the setbacks, Lillian appreciated the efforts made at Ed's junior high. She was quoted in a local newspaper saying:

> Schools here have been very, very good to us. We wouldn't want any better cooperation. When Ed first went to James Madison, Principal Roger Hamilton made copies of do's and don't's for the teachers who were to work with Eddie. The biggest thing was just to accept him as a child. It takes special work on the part of the school.[iv]

Ed spent four years at Burlington High School. For the first three, he had to use stairs to get to the bathrooms. Though he had been walking for many years by then, stairs were still a challenge, and he had to take extra time and care in using them. The school made accommodations for Ed by arranging his class schedule to minimize the need for Ed to walk up or down stairs, and by allowing him to have added time to change classes. The high school was remodeled before his senior year, and Ed had access to an elevator for that year.

In high school Ed joined the chess club where he was one of the better players. He also liked watching school athletic events.

Ed made a good friend named John French. Ed and John were the same age, but John was a few years ahead of him in school. John and his family attended the same church as the Gaines family. John's mother, Ruth, was also instrumental in Ed's life as a caregiver. When Lillian had to stay at work or if Ed needed after school care, Ruth would help. Many years later Ed received a letter from John saying that he had adopted a little boy with a physical disability, and that John believed his friendship with Ed influenced that decision.

Ed graduated from Burlington High School in 1970 at the age of 21. He was the first person with a physical disability to graduate from the school, and only a handful of people from the university hospital school to graduate from high school at all.

Ed with his parents at high school graduation. Gaines family photo collection.

2

Lillian Alvera and Richard Floyd Gaines were married November 25, 1945. Their eldest daughter Linda was born June 20, 1947. Ed was the second child, born December 12, 1948, and Barbara quickly followed November 12, 1949.

They lived in a three-bedroom apartment in Quincy, Illinois. Richard drove for the Continental Trailways Bus system. When Ed was less than a year old, Richard was transferred from Quincy, Illinois, to Burlington, Iowa. Richard would spend 30 days at a time on the road, while Lillian took care of their three kids, all younger than 3 years old. Barbara remembers a kind landlady who would help Lillian watch the kids while Richard was away. Even during the most difficult times, Barbara remembers their mother as having a sunny disposition. Ed simply calls her "wonderful."

Because the bus company went on strike, Richard was forced to take a job less suited for him as an insurance salesman for Mutual of Omaha. Once the strike was settled, he returned to Trailways, not as a driver, but as a manager.

Richard had warmth and a sense of humor, but was often bogged down by work stress and the pressure to raise his family as well as possible. The stress affected his blood pressure and made Richard more stoic.

Summers were a special time for the family. Ed would be home from the hospital school, Richard would take some time off of work, and the whole family would vacation at Tall Pines Resort near Park Rapids in northern Minnesota. Richard took the kids out on the boat to fish at Big Elbow Lake, even though Barbara says none of them wanted to touch the worms or the fish. Holding his hands two feet apart, Ed says, "We caught fish this big."

They also spent long summer days enjoying life in Burlington. At first the summers could be lonely for Ed, who was self-conscious about how his physical disabilities differentiated him from other children. The 1958 hospital school readmission note says:

> Ed's social contacts during the summer have been relatively limited. He was anxious to come back to school. The Gaines were relatively successful in getting Ed to wear his hearing aid this summer. He wore it off and on until the last few weeks of the vacation when he was informed that Judy Laness is now wearing an aid. He then seemed to want to wear his aid almost constantly.

As the summers went on, Ed continued to learn and develop social skills at the hospital school. By the next summer, his education helped him to better connect with the other kids in town:

> The parents feel Ed matured a lot and for the first time began to really socialize with children in the neighborhood. They report some difficulty getting Ed to wear his wristlets and considerable difficulty getting him to wear his anklets and feel this is due to Ed's feeling they make him appear different. He has become quite concerned about his appearance.

Ed grew up to look like Richard and started wearing his wedding ring after Richard's death in 1974. Ed was 25 years old and Richard was 59 when Richard died of a heart attack. Richard's children suspect that his high stress levels throughout their childhood may have contributed to his early death. Ed still expresses frustration that his dad's life was so short.

Lillian remarried a few years later to Lloyd "Mac" McCormick, who had worked with Richard at Trailways. Ed was happy about his mom's remarriage, in part because Mac thought Ed was funny. Mac died within one year of the marriage.

Lillian did not remarry after Mac, but continued to be active in the community. She volunteered for RSVP, Pen Pal at Earnest Horn Elementary School, Mercy Hospital gift shop, and Ronald McDonald House. She was also a dependable polling place worker for more than 15 years.

Lillian was a social catalyst even as she aged. At her first retirement home in Iowa City, she was responsible for getting a pop machine into the building as well as a flagpole out front to honor the veterans living there. When she moved, the manager missed her because she had a way of making daily experiences better for the people around her.

When Lillian died in 2014 at age 93, two car-loads of people from her retirement home attended the funeral expressing that Lillian was the person who would plan social gatherings for them. Ed was 65 when his mom died, and he continues to live in the care center where she spent her last days.

Mother and Three Kids
By Edmond R. Gaines
Written after the death of his mother

Mother gave birth to three kids,
Linda, Edmond, and Barbara,
Linda's the oldest and smartest child,
Edmond's the only child that has cerebral palsy
Due to Mother's negative blood type,
But he never gives up,
Barbara's the bookkeeping child,
Anyway, we are the happiest kids,
Because Mother did not give up on us,
Now, Mother rests in peace
After 93 years old and 66 years of hard work with us together.

3

An excerpt from "The Physical Pest: A True Story of a Man with Cerebral Palsy" by Edmond R. Gaines:

> There are many different meanings of cerebral palsy. Cerebral palsy does not fit neatly into a definition, because it affects people in so many different ways. The main term of cerebral palsy offers only a general description of a problem. Cerebral is pertaining to cerebrum and palsy can mean either paralysis (inability to move) or uncontrollable tremors. Cerebral palsy is an abnormality of the brain that interferes with the normal function of the muscles. My own terminology of cerebral palsy as the "physical pest" is because the injured cerebrum cannot control the muscles. In other words, if I drive a car and cannot control my hands and feet at the same time, then I wreck the car. If I try to hold the glass of milk and my hand is jerky sometimes, then I spill it on the floor.

> It directly affects control of the muscles. The lack of muscle control is caused by brain injury. The damage can occur before, during, or after birth. Cerebral palsy can range from mild to severe and often relates to another disability or other disabilities such as deafness, epilepsy, and/or mental retardation.

> Cerebral palsy is not a primary cause for death; it is not degenerative like multiple sclerosis or muscular dystrophy. It is not

contagious, because it is not spread from person to person like AIDS. It is not curable (lifetime disability), and it is not genetic (not inherited).

Ed's cerebral palsy occurred because of ABO incompatibility in relation to the Rh-negative factor. Lillian had the Rh-negative blood type and Richard had the Rh-positive blood type. Ed inherited the Rh-positive gene. This means that Lillian's blood did not contain the Rh protein, but Ed's did. When her body detected the Rh protein from Ed, her body attacked Ed's blood as it would a virus.

Typically, the first pregnancy for an Rh-negative mother will not cause an Rh-positive baby harm because her body will not recognize the Rh-positive proteins. During childbirth, the mother and baby's blood may interact for the first time. The mother's body develops antibodies against the Rh protein after the birth of the first child. Linda, being the first child, was not affected. When Lillian became pregnant with Ed, no one knew that Lillian's body had already developed antibodies against the Rh protein present in Ed's blood.[v]

In 1968 the FDA approved the first Rh-immune-globulin vaccinations. Since then, pregnant women are routinely checked for the Rh protein, and when a pregnant woman's blood test shows an Rh-negative blood type, she receives Rh immune-globulin shots. The shots act like a vaccination, preventing the mother's body from producing any potentially dangerous Rh antibodies. By today's medical standards, Ed's cerebral palsy was preventable.[vi]

Ed's family did not notice any health problems immediately after his birth. It was December 15, when Ed was three days old, that he began shaking. Ed's doctors discovered that he had a brain hemorrhage, which caused the brain damage that led to his cerebral palsy. Ed says, "I had to have several blood transfusions from my aunts, uncles, and father just to survive." Eighty percent of his blood was replaced through transfusion.

When Barbara was born 11 months later, Lillian's doctors were prepared for the Rh incompatibility and were able to provide the needed blood transfusions before brain damage could take place.

As Ed writes in his essay "The Physical Pest," cerebral palsy means different things for different people. Ed has both spastic and athetoid cerebral palsy. As Ed explains:

Spastic cerebral palsy involves a constant state of unusual stiffness or tension in certain muscles as if you were to loosely clench your fist and leave it clenched all day. About 67% of the people with CP have spastic. Athetoid cerebral palsy is muscle that is in constant motion. This motion may take the form of slow writhing and twisting, facial grimaces, or sudden jerks, all of which are reflex actions beyond the person's control.

When you speak with Ed, you may notice that his fists remain clenched. If you speak with him long enough, he will make sudden jerks or make a face that seems like he's in pain. Not being used to such movements, I find myself asking Ed what's wrong. He says, "Just kidding around."

Ed's early brain injury also caused deafness. Hearing impairments are not caused by cerebral palsy, but often accompany it. Ed's deafness has had as much impact on his life as his cerebral palsy, as it is his biggest barrier to communicating with others.

It's a Silent World
By Edmond R. Gaines

I see a white coyote open his mouth wide
I see ten birds perch the leafless tree
I see three church bells swing back and forth
I see five boys come to my house
I read their lips—it looks like they are singing a
Christmas carol
But it's a silent world
I do not hear the coyote howl
I do not hear ten birds trill
I do not hear three church bells chime
I do not hear five boys sing
Because I am deaf
It's a silent world.

4

Ed enrolled at Southeastern Iowa Area Community College in Burlington, Iowa, the fall after his high school graduation. The school did not provide any special accommodations, such as extra time on tests or extra notes from professors. Ed remembers that the professors would often pace the front of the room, forgetting to look at the students. Since Ed depended primarily on reading lips, he missed most of the information the teachers covered. Ed performed particularly well in the computer courses and most enjoyed his math courses.

Since Ed was older than the other students and the dorms had stairs, he lived at home while earning his degree. He didn't have access to the social aspects of college life and wasn't invited to join in any clubs.

Ed took three courses at a time and completed his Associate of Arts Degree in 1973 earning a major in business with a minor in mathematics. He also completed general education courses in English, history, and geography.

Reflecting on the great progress he made from early childhood to his college graduation, Ed wrote the poem "Miracle!"

Miracle!
Edmond R. Gaines

When I was a baby, the doctors at the hospital said to my parents,
That I was going to be a no-brain child,
Because of my brain damage,
It made my parents angry!
Then I went to the hospital school,
First I walked without the crutches or canes,
Then I talked and read people's lips,
I studied reading, 'riting and 'rithmetic!
Then I moved to the junior high school.
It had all one floor and regular students,
I chased the girls that had wonderful smiles,
The girls then went to the bathroom!
But I studied and wrote hard,
And did my best as I could and made B's and C's
Despite I didn't hear the teacher very well.
I rode a three-wheeled bike to school every day from home!
I went to the old high school for two years
It had lots of steps that I almost fell down and 'go boom'!
It became harder to read their lips,
As my teachers walked back and forth,
But like I said, "It's a miracle!"
I studied harder and harder with the supports of my friends and family,
When the new high school was built, it had steps and an elevator,
I had a special key to go the elevator,
I graduated and my parents never thought I could go all the way there!
Then I went to the older junior college (just like the older high school),
One year later they built a new junior college,
I finished my business major with math minor!
My wonderful parents and my two beautiful sisters never thought,
That I could finish,
And proud of me that I did finish it,
Wish these damned doctors here to see me alive who said I had no-brain,
"Miracle!?"
I thought so.

5

Ed's first job out of college was in 1975 as a bookkeeper at Pzazz!, a Burlington restaurant and nightclub. A few years later he worked at Hope Haven in Burlington, also as a bookkeeper.

Soon after his father's death, Ed learned to drive in a blue Ford Maverick. Barbara says Richard would not have let Ed drive if he had been alive. Within three months of Ed receiving his license, Ed had three car accidents. Lillian would come home to find policemen at the house. Ed's basic driving abilities were fine, but he didn't have the reflexes to respond to unforeseen events. After the third accident, Ed and his family agreed that Ed would no longer drive.

In 1981, Ed says, "I moved to Iowa City out my own."

He started as a bookkeeper and computer operator at Goodwill and lived in a group home. Ed would take himself to work at Goodwill on a 3-wheeled bike. One day his bike caught on railroad tracks. Ed fell and cracked three ribs. Barbara went to Ed's house at the group home soon after the fall and walked in on Ed's counselor berating him for trying to get out of doing the dishes. Barbara started looking for new housing.

Ed on his three-wheeled bike. Gaines family photo collection.

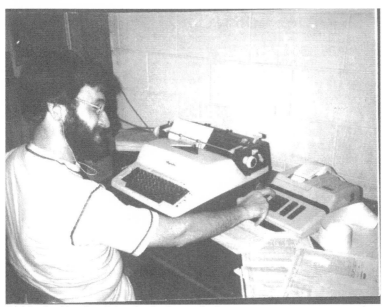

Ed doing bookkeeping. Gaines family photo collection.

That's when Ed's family met Tom Walz, a professor of social work at the University of Iowa. Walz helped Ed secure a new housing situation at the Ecumenical Towers. Ed became one of its first residents when it opened near the end of 1981. The Ecumenical Towers was the result of a 7-year movement to build affordable housing for elderly people. Ed had his own handicap apartment. It was the most independent living situation he had ever had. Lillian also lived in the Ecumenical Towers from 1985-1993 before deciding to move back to Burlington so that Ed would have more independence.

Walz also connected Ed with Wild Bill's Coffeeshop, a service learning project operated by adults with disabilities housed with The University of Iowa School of Social Work.

Wild Bill's gets its name from Bill Sackter, a man who spent 44 years in a Minnesota mental institution for a life-long mental disability before becoming a local Iowa City celebrity. After being discharged from the Faribault State Hospital, Sackter became friends with college student Barry Morrow. When Morrow accepted a job at the School of Social Work at the University of Iowa, he put Sackter in charge of a small coffee service in North Hall, which houses the School of Social Work. Sackter's cheerful demeanor, good will, and harmonica gained him popularity in Iowa City. Morrow would go on to co-write a television movie about Sackter's life, which made Wild Bill's Coffeeshop famous.[vii]

When Sackter died in 1983, Ed became part of the three-person team that came in to take over Sackter's duties. Ed worked with David Young and Beverly McClelland for eight years at Wild Bill's. Like Sackter, both Young and McClelland had histories of unnecessary institutionalization that brought undue burden to their lives. In a 1984 newspaper article appearing in The Cedar Rapids Gazette, McClelland said that being able to take a role at the coffeeshop was, "a second chance."[viii] The opportunity to work at Wild Bill's Coffeeshop was exciting for all of them. Ed says that Sackter was a hero for pioneering entrepreneurial opportunities for people with disabilities in Iowa.

Bill Sackter, A National Hero
By Edmond R. Gaines

Everyone talked about how Bill had a wonderful life
To me, Bill Sackter was a hero, How?
He set the people with all disabilities free!
By talking on the TV and going to the public

He was not afraid anywhere he went
They should nationally put April to honor him
People with disabilities of the month
Just like February heart of the month
Or Mother's in May or Father's Day in June.

Ed gave up walking at age 35 after falling too many times. After that he travelled by electric wheelchair.

In 1991 at age 42, Ed embarked on his first original entrepreneurial pursuit. Mr. Ed's Coffee Shop was housed in what used to be the International Building at the University of Iowa, currently the College of Public Health Building. The opening of the coffee shop was publicized in several newspaper articles. *The Daily Iowan* quoted Ed as saying, "I opened the shop because I wanted to gain some independence. It is for self-esteem and pride."ix

When Ed had previously sought employment in Iowa City, he found some businesses to be unsupportive in hiring a person with disabilities. This took place even after the Americans with Disabilities Act was passed in 1990. Although the ADA made strides toward greater accommodations for people with disabilities in the workplace, it still allows businesses to make their own assessments of whether or not hiring a person with a disability would place undue hardship on their businesses: "Undue hardship means that the accommodation would be too difficult or too expensive to provide, in light of the employer's size, financial resources, and the needs of the business."x Although Ed had already proven to be an effective bookkeeper for several small Iowa businesses, employers still had the freedom to choose not to hire him based on their individual assessments of his needs.

Part of Ed's mission in opening the coffee shop became hiring other people with disabilities. At the time Mr. Ed's Coffee Shop opened, he had hired five people with disabilities along with a job coach. Mr. Ed's provided lunch options for people working and studying in the International Center and a place to relax or play chess between classes. Mr. Ed's also sold antiques and used books.

Ed created a warm and comfortable atmosphere for people to enjoy. Ed and some of the shop's regulars started a joke that they were "Ed Heads." They posted a sign in the coffee shop that described an Ed Head as "a person who demonstrates scholarly interest and abilities; who reflects an appreciation of cultural difference; and who exemplifies compassion for others, particularly those in greatest need." While the "Ed Heads" group

Ed and a friend at Mr. Ed's. Gaines family photo collection.

was a joke between friends, it was also a good description of the values that Ed spread through his entrepreneurship.

In a nomination letter to the Goodwill of the Heartland's 1992 Emily Helms Award Committee, Tom Walz describes Mr. Ed's Coffee Shop:

> One only needs to visit Mr. Ed's to appreciate the creative touch he has given it. From his definition of Ed Heads to his computer graphics used to advertise his specials, one becomes aware of his humor, talent, and goal directedness. Ed clearly has as part of his mission to educate the non-handicapped about the world of handicapped persons.

Walz concludes the letter with high praise of Ed's character and capabilities as an individual:

> In truth he has contributed far more to us than we have to him. Ed is a determined, tenacious, but positive individual. The good things that have happened to him have come from his own doing. He is independent and responsible, a model to both handicapped and non handicapped alike. I've learned a lot from Ed and grown in my respect for him.

Ed was selected as the winner of the Emily Helms Award in 1992 for his business endeavors. The award recognizes individuals with significant disabilities who "demonstrate outstanding strength of character" with "courage, perseverance, industry, humor, imagination, and leadership."[xi]

It was during this time that Ed moved to the old Press Citizen Building. The building was newly renovated to make low-income housing for elderly people and people with disabilities. Ed moved there to receive more assistance. Barbara says that it was the best living situation Ed had in Iowa City. Ed had revolving help with cooking, cleaning, shopping, and laundry.

While the Press Citizen building was a great idea, some people who were employed to help him took advantage of the situation and bought groceries for themselves with Ed's money. This coincided with similar challenges at Mr. Ed's Coffee Shop, which had to close after just two years.

Ed faced many challenges as the proprietor of Mr. Ed's Coffee Shop. Basic business communications proved difficult to maneuver, as Ed's hearing disability made it impossible for him to speak on the phone, and he had a difficult time communicating with customers. The coffee shop was also not in a high-traffic area of Iowa City, and it was too inconvenient for people who were not already involved with the International Building to visit.

While communication and location where difficult trials for the coffee shop, issues with theft presented the worst challenges. Ed submitted a letter to the editor of *The Daily Iowan* addressing the issue:

> Two years ago, I opened a small coffee shop in the International Center. In these two years I have had my cash register stolen twice, along with the theft of some merchandise. Thanks to the help of some high-school volunteers who work with Campus Security, the cash registers were recovered, though badly damaged. They had been thrown into a neighboring pond.
>
> Unfortunately, the coffee shop is without security, as the doors must remain open as a fire-safety measure. If anyone who may have been involved reads this, I'd like to ask them to be more understanding. I am a severely handicapped person who suffers from cerebral palsy and earn very little at the coffee shop. Recently, I have introduced used books to augment the small food sales. These books are without protection. I don't know what I would do if I were to experience more theft or vandalism. Thank you for your consideration. I welcome your visits.

Despite the early anticipation and excitement expressed in multiple newspapers for Mr. Ed's Coffee Shop, the business had to close.

Ed quickly tried again with a new business model: Mr. Ed's SuperGraphics. Ed produced posters, flyers, and business cards. He started the business in North Hall, near Wild Bill's Coffeeshop, but when a new dean started at the college in 2000, the dean asked Mr. Ed's SuperGraphics to leave because of its status as a for-profit business.

Tom Walz contacted Gerald Sorokin who directed Hillel, a jewish faith community at the University of Iowa, to find a new home for Mr. Ed's SuperGraphics at Hillel. Sorokin describes the arrangement as a win-win, wherein "Ed had free access to space (and a color printer) in a centrally-located facility; the Hillel students had the chance to interact with Ed, learn about his publishing work, and observe how he managed his disability." During that time, Hillel also received a grant from Iowa City that allowed them to renovate the restrooms to be handicap accessible.

Meanwhile, Tom Walz was working on another endeavor to advance entrepreneurial options for people with disabilities, which he called the Extend The Dream Foundation. Extend The Dream used Wild Bill's Coffeeshop as inspiration with the goal of extending entrepreneurial opportunities to more people. Through the foundation Walz secured funding and the assistance of three AmeriCorps VISTAs to create Uptown Bill's Small Mall of micro-businesses owned by people with disabilities. As soon as the space was ready in 2001, Mr. Ed's SuperGraphics moved to Uptown Bill's Small Mall.[xii]

Mr. Ed's SuperGraphics was open for a total of 10 years. Ed had an industrial-sized printer. He designed and printed business cards, flyers, and posters. His friends and clients called Ed "The God of Clipart." Communication continued to be a setback for Ed's business, but he had the help of volunteers and social work students from the university. At Mr. Ed's SuperGraphics, Ed was able to create a space that was comfortable for him and patrons of his business.

In the early 2000's Extend the Dream continued to advocate for the independence of people with disabilities through the purchase of a Universal Designed home dubbed The Bill Sackter House. The house provided space for three residents with disabilities and a caretaker. The residents, including Ed and Leo Huisman, who also had cerebral palsy, were the official homeowners.

The purchase was possible in part because of a collaborative effort by Extend the Dream, the Iowa City Council, the Housing Authority, and Mercy Hospital, which donated $40,000 toward the purchase.[xiii]

The Bill Sackter House was the first Universal Designed home in Iowa City. Universal Design is a concept that moves beyond accessible or barrier-free housing in that it is designed to exceed standards for handicap accessibility while also providing space that is suitable for everyone. The hope behind Universal Design is that it will become a standard practice in home building, as it recognizes that most of the features needed by people with disabilities are also useful to others.[xiv] For example, larger bathrooms and wider doorways provide a more comfortable experience for everyone. Universal Design also recognizes that many able-bodied people eventually will age and find need for wheelchairs or other accommodations.

Living in the Bill Sackter House gave Ed the experience of homeownership and an independent living space. The start of the project proved challenging as the first caretaker had family needs that precluded him from fulfilling the needs of the household, and it took some time to find the right person for the job. Ed also had roommates come and go. His favorite roommates were Gretchen Gentsch and Ricky Chacon. Gentsch also ran a business out of the small mall. The three cared for a cat and a small dog.

Ed lived in the house for nearly 10 years before it became too difficult for him to maintain. Between a bedbug infestation, painful nerve damage from hitting his elbow while crossing railroad tracks, and more challenges that came as Ed was aging, Ed needed more assistance and greater access to nurses to keep him healthy.

In 2013, through the Reach For Your Potential program, Ed moved to a group home. He was there for just longer than a year, but he was struck by another resident, and the entire situation felt like a disaster. From there he relocated to the nursing home where his mother was living at the time.

In any other city in Iowa, Barbara says, Ed would not have had the resources to live as independently as he has. Iowa City provided wheelchair friendly city buses, volunteer assistance, and physical accommodations in buildings. As Ed aged, he received assistance from the Arc of Southeast Iowa, a program dedicated to advocacy and welfare of individuals with disabilities. The University of Iowa was also a huge resource, connecting experts in the field of social work with local citizens.

For the final leg of his career, Ed became the manager of Uptown Bill's Coffeeshop, an extension of the North Hall coffeeshop housed in the Wild Bill's Small Mall. Ed retired in 2014 at age 65. By the time of his retirement he had invested more than 30 years in the Wild Bill's Coffeeshop legacy.

The Old Man and The Coffeeshop
by Edmond R. Gaines

The old man enters a well-known coffeeshop
He is handsome and "a wild and crazy guy"
He jokes and teases people
He has a wonderful voice that sounds like Bing
He sings wild and crazy songs
In the coffeeshop, it has a friendly atmosphere
The people are wonderful there
They like to laugh and smile.
The students from the great university are learning about
the way of life of people with disabilities
Especially the old man who has cerebral palsy and hearing loss.
The old man is me.

6

I met Ed near the end of his time at The Bill Sackter House. He was 64 and I was 22. Right away I learned that he was a chess-player and writer. He also gave me a big smile and told me, "I'm a sunshine guy."

My responsibilities in working with him were to take care of his needs, which changed throughout the year I spent with him. One consistent routine task was pouring caffeine-free, diet Mountain Dew from cans into bottles through a funnel. This task had developed because Ed loved Mountain Dew, but stopped drinking caffeine for his heart health, and switched to diet to help keep a healthy weight. As it turns out, caffeine-free, diet Mountain Dew was only sold in cans at the time, but it was too difficult for Ed to control a can with his cerebral palsy. Thus, the funnel.

I also shaved his face, clipped his toenails, brushed his teeth, ran his errands, swept his floors, dusted his model cars, cleaned his toilets, cleaned his keyboard, and we talked.

Ed talked about never having a long-term girlfriend. Sometimes he would talk about it in the form of jokes. Other times he would try to understand why it had never happened for him. He believed it was because women were scared to marry someone with a disability. He talked about how he couldn't perform all the same tasks as a person without cerebral palsy, and specifically how he couldn't hold a baby because he might drop it when he experienced a muscle tremor.

My time with Ed was during the 2012 presidential campaign. He often had coverage of the race between the incumbent President Barack Obama and the Republican nominee, Mitt Romney, playing on television. The coverage would sometimes make him so mad his face would turn red. Ed had a lot to say about the political situation in the United States and never held back his opinion.

Ed's political opinions were formed from his life experiences. As a person who worked every day for the independence he held, Ed still relied on government aid. During my time working with him, food stamp rations were reduced, and Ed had to find ways to make up the difference in his already tight budget.

Ed's ability to get to work was affected by government decisions. At some points in his life he qualified for brain injury waivers that allowed him to have free access to city buses that would take him to work. At other times, he would not qualify for brain injury waivers and would have to figure out how to get to work himself.

Ed's entire life, from the time he started school, was shaped by the laws and resources that the state and federal governments were willing to provide. There were points when he felt like the politicians making decisions for him didn't care if he lived or died.

> *Our Land of the Free and Our Home of the Brave*
> By Edmond R. Gaines
>
> *We, the people, have forgotten the song written by a man named Francis Scott Key. He wrote our national anthem called The Star Spangled Banner. The last statement is beautiful. "O'er the land of the free and the home of the brave." Now we have problems with our government. They have forgotten Thomas Jefferson's ideas. His ideas were freedom, equality, and justice for all. He talked about all people, not just 99% and not just 1% people. Our government is divided and not united. Because of the wrong people, they think money comes first rather than helping all people. I would say to all members of the Congress "People come first, because it's our land of the free and our home of the brave."*

Even as Ed and his family continually figured out changing regulations around the resources the government provided him, Ed also had regular daily-life challenges to meet.

I was working with Ed when bedbugs first started leaving red welts up and down his arms. Barbara tried to move Ed to a nursing home, but no one would take him because they were afraid that he would bring bedbugs with him. His family helped him to wash and store all of his belongings, the bedbugs were exterminated, and Ed was able to continue living in the home.

Soon after the bedbugs, Ed developed bed sores, and I accompanied him to the emergency room, where the nurses worked to keep his fragile skin together. After that, I spent much more of my time with Ed helping him to change bandages.

After one year of working at the Arc my angst to use my college education became too strong, and I gave my two-week notice. Within that one year, I felt like I had been through a lot with Ed. When I told him I was leaving, he looked upset and asked me why. I said it was so I could make some money. He didn't care for that answer.

Ed kept asking me why I was leaving throughout the two weeks, until we were sitting face to face and I pointed to my head and said I wanted to use my brain. His facial expression changed from frustration to excitement. "Oh! You want a brain job, like me!" Ed understood. As a person whose self-sufficiency came through mental work, he understood my desire to use my college education at work.

In the years that followed, I still thought of Ed, missed him, and thought of how I had promised to write his life story and never followed through. After a three and a half year stint as a marketing writer for a small college, I realized that I didn't just promise to write Ed's life story, I wanted to.

I emailed Ed hoping he was still willing. He didn't remember that I had said I would write it, but he did remember me. As I learned more about Ed's story, my excitement to write it grew, and I became more in awe of Ed.

Ed doesn't just live with cerebral palsy. He makes a mission to live independently, to teach people about his disability, and to advocate for the independence and unity of all people.

Open My Mind and Open My Heart
by Edmond R. Gaines

I open my mind and open my heart to feel free
Free from fear! Fear not of my disability
I hope that someday I will be totally free
I believe I have faith to someone
Why? Because I love you as a friend
I'm in love with someone
Someone loves me so true
I'm in love with someone

In the coffeeshop I saw you coming
Oh, how I see your wonderful smile
Will you sit by my side and be my friend
We are under the rainbow sky
We will remember Iowa City
I'm in love with someone
Someone loves me so true
I'm in love with someone

A Note On Editing

While it is an unusual practice to publish anything that does not follow formal grammar, I decided that editing Ed's words would sterilize them and strip them of his personality.

At times Ed's writing is careful and patient, reflective of his practice in chess, like in "Sixty-Four" or "It's A Silent World." Other times his writing exudes emotion and energy, like in "Miracle!" When I read "Miracle!" I picture Ed speaking quickly and excitedly about his accomplishments, with the animated gestures that only Ed could produce.

REFERENCES

[i] Jackie Maxwell, "Parents advised: Take him out and let him go," June 22, 1970, *Burlington Hawk Eye.*

[ii] Jackie Maxwell, "Parents advised: Take him out and let him go," June 22, 1970, *Burlington Hawk Eye.*

[iii] Paul B. McCray, Jr., M.D., "A history of the department of pediatrics University of Iowa Hospitals & Clinics: 1870 -1986," 1987, The University of Iowa.

[iv] Jackie Maxwell, "Parents advised: Take him out and let him go," June 22, 1970, *Burlington Hawk Eye.*

[v] "What is cerebral palsy?" February 2017, retrieved from https://www.cerebralpalsyguide.com/cerebral-palsy/

[vi] "What is cerebral palsy?" February 2017, retrieved from https://www.cerebralpalsyguide.com/cerebral-palsy/

[vii] "Wild Bill's Coffeeshop," retrieved October 2017, from https://clas.uiowa.edu/socialwork/resources/wild-bills-coffeeshop

[viii] Karen Herzog, "Wild Bill's serves up a second chance," February 5, 1984, *The Cedar Rapids Gazette.*

[ix] Alan Goldis, "Coffee, cookies, 'Ed-Heads'—'Mr. Ed's' has grand opening," April 17, 1991, *The Daily Iowan*, pg. 3A.

[x] "Disability discrimination," U.S. Equal Employment Opportunity Commission, retrieved October 2017, from https://www.eeoc.gov/laws/types/disability.cfm

[xi] "Goodwill seeks Emily Helms Award nominations," February 20, 2014, retrieved from https://www.goodwillheartland.org/news-release/goodwill-seeks-emily-helms-award-nominations

[xii] Sarah Hankel, "Uptown Bill's Small Mall to open in July," May 30, 2001, *Community News Advertiser*, pg. 3.

xiii Deidre Bello, "Locals mark ADA," July 28, 2002, *Iowa City Press Citizen.*

xiv Ronald L. Mace, "Universal Design in Housing," retrieved October 2017 from https://www.humancentereddesign.org/resources/universal-design-housing

ABOUT THE AUTHOR

Summer Gaasedelen developed a passion for creative writing while attending St. Olaf College in Northfield, Minnesota. She gained experience writing short biographies during her time as a marketing writer at Cornell College in Mount Vernon, Iowa. This is Gaasedelen's first full-length biography and first independent book publication.

Made in the USA
Monee, IL
09 December 2020

51710885R00028